PLAY AND REFLECTION
IN DONALD WINNICOTT'S
WRITINGS

THE DONALD WINNICOTT MEMORIAL LECTURE

PLAY AND REFLECTION IN DONALD WINNICOTT'S WRITINGS

Given by

André Green

Published by
KARNAC
on behalf of
THE WINNICOTT CLINIC OF PSYCHOTHERAPY
Registered Charity No. 260427

Published in 2005 by
Karnac (Books) Ltd.
6 Pembroke Buildings, London NW10 6RE
on behalf of
The Winnicott Clinic of Psychotherapy
PO Box 233
Ruislip
HA4 8UJ

British Library Cataloguing in Publication Data

A C.I.P. for this book is available from the British Library

  ISBN 1 85575 387 1

Edited, designed, and produced by The Studio Publishing Services Ltd, Exeter EX4 8JN

Printed in Great Britain

www.karnacbooks.com

CONTENTS

CONTRIBUTORS

André Green is a training analyst of the Paris Psychoanalytic Society and an Honorary Member of the British Psychoanalytical Society. He is a Patron of the Squiggle Foundation. He is the author of various books published in the field of psychoanalysis, among others *Chains of Eros*, *On Private Madness*, *Work of the Negative*, and *Time in Psychoanalysis*.

Brett Kahr is Senior Clinical Research Fellow in Psychotherapy and Mental Health at the Centre for Child Mental Health in London, and the Winnicott Clinic Senior Research Fellow in Psychotherapy at the Winnicott Clinic of Psychotherapy. He is also Visiting Clinician at the Tavistock Centre for Couple Relationships, part of the Tavistock Institute of Medical Psychology. He has written or edited several books on Winnicott, notably *D. W. Winnicott: A Biographical Portrait*, which received the Gradiva Prize for Biography in 1997, as well as *Forensic Psychotherapy and Psychopathology: Winnicottian Perspectives*, and *The Legacy of Winnicott: Essays on Infant and Child Mental Health*, all published by Karnac Books. He is also a Patron of the Squiggle Foundation, and an Adviser to the Winnicott Clinic of Psychotherapy. Most recently, he has become the Resident

Psychotherapist on BBC Radio 2, and Spokesperson for the BBC initiative "Life 2 Live".

Eric Koops, LVO, is the Chairman of the Trustees of the Winnicott Clinic of Psychoanalysis, the registered charity responsible for the annual Donald Winnicott Memorial Lecture.

The Clinic was founded in 1969 to promote professional training in the principles of psychotherapy, to conduct research, and to assist in the provision of individual psychotherapy. During the 1990s, to meet changing circumstances, assistance was extended to patients in group therapy, training grants were awarded, and symposia arranged to encourage organizations to reduce workplace stress.

Since 2000, the main focus of Clinic activities has been the wider dissemination of the work and ideas of Dr Donald W. Winnicott (1896–1971), the distinguished English paediatrician, child psychiatrist, and psychoanalyst, who made an outstanding contribution to the understanding of the causes of mental illness, particularly in infants and children. To this end, the Clinic established the Winnicott Clinic Senior Research Fellowship in Psychotherapy and Counselling, and the annual Donald Winnicott Memorial Lecture, designed for a wide audience of professionals and others involved with children. Lectures focus upon specific topics arising from Winnicott's life and ideas, in terms of relevance for twenty-first century living.

Foreword

Eric Koops

I t is my great pleasure to welcome you to this, the third Donald Winnicott Memorial Lecture. We are very pleased to see so many, especially many who were here last year, and some who were here two years ago. To us, this third Lecture is really something of a milestone. We have a partnership with Karnac Books, by whom both previous Lectures have been published—as we intend that tonight's will be.

We are a small charity, but we think that this dissemination is a critical educational factor for us and for those around. We also recognize that an annual lecture of this sort provides a meeting-point for people. Some of you may not have seen each other for months, or even a year, and we would welcome any feedback that you might like to give us—perhaps, for example, whether or not we as a Clinic might do a little more to foster meetings of this nature, acting as a catalyst for those who are often really quite "lonely" out there in the field.

Having welcomed you, my next tasks are very simple: to ask Brett Kahr to introduce our speaker, and to assure you that we are very conscious that many of you will need to get away at the time stated on the ticket application in order to catch last trains home.

Introduction

Brett Kahr

Good evening, ladies and gentlemen. No doubt many of you here tonight, if not all of you, will be familiar with the wonderful bronze statue of Sigmund Freud, created by the sculptor Oscar Nemon, that sat for many years beside the library in Swiss Cottage in North London. In more recent years, the statue has been relocated, and it now resides in a little garden nook in front of the Tavistock Clinic, not far from the Freud Museum. Although colleagues will know this statue quite well, it may not be appreciated that Donald Winnicott, the man to whom we pay tribute this evening, played a leading role in having Nemon's statue of Freud set in bronze and unveiled at a special ceremony on 2 October 1970, only a few months before Winnicott's own death from cardiac disease on 25 January 1971. Winnicott expended a great deal of energy during his final months of illness to ensure that sufficient funds would be raised so that his great hero, Sigmund Freud, could be properly memorialized.

Just as Winnicott helped us to remember Freud, tonight we have gathered here to remember Winnicott, a man whose contributions to psychotherapy and psychoanalysis, and whose understanding of children, remains unparalleled. When those of us associated with the Winnicott Clinic of Psychotherapy decided how this should be accomplished, we opted not for a statue, but rather for something living and breathing and very vibrant, in keeping with Donald Winnicott's own character (Kahr, 1996). Following in the distinguished footsteps of Dr Joyce McDougall, our first Winnicott Memorial lecturer, and Sir Richard Bowlby, our second Winnicott Memorial lecturer, we have really struck psychoanalytical gold: Professor André Green of Paris has honoured us by accepting our invitation to deliver the Third Annual Donald Winnicott Memorial Lecture, and to talk to us this evening about his reflections on Winnicott's theory of play.

Born in Cairo in 1927, to a Sephardi Jewish family originally known as "Gren", André Green, the youngest of four children, emigrated to France in 1946 to undertake his university studies. He decided upon a career in medicine and psychiatry at quite an early age, and after arriving in Paris on 8 May 1946, he set about his plan with gusto. In a recent interview, Professor Green recalled that:

> The teaching of medicine was very boring. For the first years, I was a bad student. I didn't pay much attention to my exams and I used to work for myself; I studied philosophy, psychology; I read books about culture, not very useful for my medical training. [Quoted in Green & Kohon, 1999b, p. 15]

One can already identify the early signs that for Green, medicine and psychiatry would prove to be a gateway to his ultimate profession of psychoanalysis.

André Green undertook his psychiatric training at the renowned Parisian hospital, the Hôpital Sainte Anne, under the tutelage of the eminent psychiatrist, Professor Henri Ey, whose name may not be familiar to an Anglo-Saxon readership today, but who, during the 1950s, "was indisputably the most important figure of psychiatry in France, and maybe even in the world" (quoted in Green & Kohon, 1999b, p. 17). It may well have been Dr Green's experience of working with Professor Ey that afforded that privileged insight into the dynamics of the more troubled and more complex patients with whom André Green has worked so closely during the last four or more decades.

In the early 1950s, as a young psychiatrist, Green began to find his way to psychoanalysis—by no means an easy undertaking for a

French psychiatrist at that time, as psychoanalysis had not then captured the cultural imagination of France as it would do in the period from 1968 onwards. In fact, André Green will remember the mid-century discovery of two French biomedical researchers who recognized the sedative properties of a class of drugs called phenothiazines, especially chlorpromazine, which ushered in the pharmacological revolution, not only in French psychiatry, but worldwide. To have had the courage and independence of mind to find one's way to psychoanalysis just as the rest of the psychiatric profession became so pharmacologically orientated, gives us an indication of André Green's strength of character, and of his ability to remain his own man.

He began his personal analysis in 1956 with the highly respected French psychoanalyst Maurice Bouvet, himself the student of Sacha Nacht, one of the earliest Parisian psychoanalysts. Green completed his analysis in 1960, shortly before Bouvet's death. He then undertook two more analyses, first with Jean Mallet, and then with Catherine Parat (Etchegoyen, 1999a), qualifying as a member of the Société Psychanalytique de Paris, the oldest psychoanalytical society in France. Since the completion of his studies, Green has had a most distinguished career in all aspects of psychoanalysis, having served as President of the Société Psychanalytique de Paris, Director of the Institut de Psychanalyse, as well as having served as Vice-President of the International Psycho-Analytical Association. He also held high offices for *The International Journal of Psycho-Analysis* and the *Nouvelle Revue de Psychanalyse*.

No stranger to Great Britain, many of you will recall that Professor Green held the Freud Memorial Professorship at University College London during the 1979–1980 academic year, and he has visited the Squiggle Foundation in London on many occasions. He has authored a large number of books on a variety of topics over many decades, each characterized by a unique writing style, full of classical and literary references that draw upon Green's great intelligence and vast erudition.

Although trained as a classical psychoanalyst, Green remains one of the few traditional French psychoanalysts who studied the work of Jacques Lacan with great seriousness, at a time when Lacan's more conservative colleagues regarded him as mad. Similarly, André Green championed the work of Donald Winnicott long before most continental psychoanalysts had begun to develop an appreciation for the great English psychoanalyst. Though one may not easily detect overt correspondences between the work of Lacan and Winnicott, I think that Green's appreciation for these two psychoanalytical titans provides us with more evidence of his independent-mindedness, for not many people could have had profitable dialogues with both Lacan and with Winnicott. Among contemporary practitioners, André Green, perhaps more than almost anyone, epitomizes an international spirit of independence, which Donald Winnicott would so much have appreciated.

It gives me great pleasure, ladies and gentlemen, that Professor André Green has come from Paris to speak to us tonight, and I now call upon him to deliver the Third Annual Donald Winnicott Memorial Lecture.

References

Etchegoyen, R. H. (1999a). Preface. In: G. Kohon (Ed.), *The Dead Mother: The Work of André Green* (pp. xi–xxiii). London: Routledge.

Green, A., & Kohon, G. (1999b). The Greening of psychoanalysis: André Green in dialogues with Gregorio Kohon. In: G. Kohon (Ed.), *The Dead Mother: The Work of André Green* (pp. 10–58). London: Routledge.

Kahr, B. (1996). *D. W. Winnicott: A Biographical Portrait*. London: Karnac.

Play and reflection in Donald Winnicott's writings

André Green

In writing Donald Winnicott's commemoration I find that I strongly identify with him. Throughout his life Winnicott struggled against compliance, conformism, and submission. It is scarcely surprising there has not been any Winnicottian school and that no one is called his disciple, even those closest to him. As I feel a certain continuity exists between Winnicott and myself, I shall not provide a submissive account of his ideas, even though I do think he was the most creative mind in psychoanalysis, after Freud.

When Winnicott gave his first lecture to the British Psychoanalytical Society, on 28 November 1945, on the subject of "Primitive emotional development", he said it was like the introduction to a book. He expounded his original method: ideas were not formed from other theories. He confessed that in building his own theory, he gathered elements from various sources and "related them to his clinical experience", but was prepared to examine in due course the few things he "stole" here and there from others. However, my concern here is not what Winnicott is said to have "stolen" from others, but rather what his own theory chose to leave out and would not embrace.

Today I am going to talk about Winnicott's last work, which I consider a sort of testament: *Playing and Reality* (1971). I shall focus attention mainly on playing and not so much on reality—despite Winnicott's locating play, like other transitional phenomena, between inner and outer reality; outer reality does not seem to me limited to objectively perceived objects. I think it is in the presence of horror that we understand the necessity of play in making it bearable.

Winnicott had been interested in play ever since 1942 (*Why Children Play*) but I am more interested in his last statements about it. Two central chapters are devoted to play in *Playing and Reality*. One of them, "Playing: a theoretical statement", is constantly quoted at length and is considered to be the most detailed study on the topic. The other chapter, "Playing: creative activity and the search of the self", is, quite surprisingly, almost never mentioned; maybe it provokes little comment because it is obscure and difficult. Although the two chapters are very different it is my feeling that, bearing the same title, they must be tightly linked. I shall consider this two-sided development as the axis of my elaboration. I believe that many of the other chapters of the book, whether before or after this central couple, are enlightened by reference to them.

First, I want to make a statement to indicate where I stand. On the one hand I accept the profound originality and the creativity of most of the concepts introduced by Winnicott in psychoanalysis; on the other, I disagree with Winnicott's explanation of their supposed origin in the mother–baby relationship.

I think that it was thanks to Winnicott's experience of the analytic situation—and we perhaps may say his own experience first as an analysand—that he was able, when looking at children, to notice what had been escaping everyone else's attention.

In *Human Nature* (1988), a book published posthumously, when considering the earliest stages, Winnicott moves towards the complete merging of the individual and the environment that is implied in the words "primary narcissism". Winnicott compares it with the physical transformation of the endometrium intermingled with the placenta. This basic hypothesis appears to me as a fecundity for the later construction of transitional phenomena to which play is so closely linked:

There is an intermediate state between this and interpersonal relationships which has very great importance of which it could be said
that between the mother who is physically holding the baby and
the baby there is a layer which, we have to acknowledge, is an
aspect of herself and at the same time an aspect of the baby. It is
mad to hold this view and yet this view must be maintained.
[Winnicott, 1988]

Let us consider this quotation. I think of it as what we may call the
"unsaid" in Winnicott; something that he did not publish—yet all
that he published derives from this basic hypothesis that, curiously,
we do not find in his work. Everything he wrote on the transitional
alternative area, the transitional phenomena and the symbolic
union, is grounded in this "mad" view of something belonging at
the same time to the mother and to the child. This, of course, poses
questions for our ideas on identity and on the meaning of trying to
reunite what has been separated.

I think it may be a surprise for many of you to see how I dissoc-
iate myself from this point of view. I believe that as a paediatrician
Winnicott could not free himself from this viewpoint; he was deter-
mined to see things like that. However, I do not think, for instance,
that playing is rooted in, or deeply influenced by, the mother–baby
relationship.

That concept is one which Winnicott would not consider important in analysis with his adult patients—and probably in his own—
and that is what created some misunderstandings, or some
regrettable lacunae, in his theory. Such gaps, in my view, were
shared with many other authors in the British Society. One such
gap, for instance, is Winnicott's dismissal of the part of sexuality in
playing. At the beginning of the chapter "Playing: a theoretical
statement", Winnicott devotes a rather extensive section to the
(negative) relationship between play and masturbation: "There is
one thing I want to get out of the way" (Winnicott, 1988). He argues
about the physical excitement of play, yet rejects the links in our
mind between playing and masturbatory activity. He believes that
"if, when a child is playing, the physical excitement of instinctual
involvement becomes evident, then the playing stops". He does not
consider that the stopping of the play could be preventive of
orgasm or equivalent to it. He does not think of the comparison

between play and foreplay where, too, if the excitement is over-whelming, what we have is premature ejaculation, which brings an end to the sexual relationship. Moreover, Winnicott seems to ignore Freud's concept of aim-inhibited drives, a very surprising matter since he develops at length the relationship between playing and friendship just as Freud did; he, for his part, quotes the same example: "friendship as an expression on aim-inhibited drives". It is striking to see how much energy Winnicott spends in dissociating playing from sexuality. Ever since the time of Melanie Klein, around the 1930s, sexuality has been considered by British analysts as a secondary and rather unimportant matter, except in the case of perversions. Winnicott, therefore, recommends on the subject the works of those who are not analysts. Let me point out that Winnicott refuses the hypothesis of a preliminary or primary form of sublimation.

Though there may be a great deal to say about this—as can be inferred from biographies of Winnicott, as Rodman so excellently demonstrates—I shall systematically neglect all arguments related to his historical background and personality. If I disagree with the explanation grounded in the mother–baby relationship, I am not going to interpret Winnicott's ideas according to this baby and mother relationship, however eloquent are the details we possess and their possible influence on Winnicott according to his own confessions to his friends.

My feeling about the importance of play in Winnicott is related to the fact that Winnicott himself was of a very playful nature. He once said of himself that he was "a clown" and that he understood how important it was to himself to have play as a remedy for his helplessness towards reality.

In the excellent compilations about playing in the works of Winnicott (for example, those by Alexander Newman and Jan Abram) different aspects related to that concept are described. I do not intend to re-examine the relationship of playing to these aspects, but will rather try to clarify what appear to me as the more fundamental characteristics as I see them.

I agree with Winnicott, at least partly, when he writes: "*It is play that is the universal* and that belongs to health. . . . The natural thing is playing and the highly sophisticated twentieth century phenomena is psychoanalysis" (Winnicott, 1971).

The first words of the quotation are emphasized. I totally share this opinion. There is no culture without play; there are no periods of history from which play has been absent. But if it is so, and I believe it is, this universality is compatible with all the varieties of mother–baby relationships, either in the different phases of history or in the different cultures on earth, although play is constantly present everywhere.

My conclusion, therefore, is that play, this universal activity, belongs to an innate attribute of the mind that takes different shapes, not only in various groups, but also for different individuals. Winnicott was too stuck in the mother–baby relationship to interpret its universality in relationship to the characteristics of the mind. I am not even sure that play belongs to health. For example, I wonder how health can be integral to some kinds of play—such as the Roman games, or playing a kind of football with the heads of the defeated enemies in Latin America, or playing Russian roulette; today, even football matches may become excuses for assassinations. On the other hand, I see a strong participation of the drives, both sexual and destructive. I wonder how Winnicott would have interpreted the shouts of joy, the enthusiasm, the orgasmic quality which accompanies the cry of "Goal!" I doubt health has anything to do with that. I think the activity of play can sometimes become distorted, corrupted and perverted, in society as well as in individuals: e.g., *Panem et circenses*.

Here I am afraid that on this occasion, as on many others, we meet Winnicott's idealization and his refusal to consider play as part of sickness. I think Winnicott was wrong in mixing up "ruthless love" with what was sheer destruction, and also in being so reticent about admitting the death instinct hypothesis. I cannot prove the existence of a death instinct (though some recent biological discoveries—"apoptosis"—do seem to favour it). But what I am sure of is that it is not enough to incarnate the good-mother to cure a patient, to vanish when she acts out her destructivity, or to accept passively the patient's destroying the setting. Sometimes the analyst cheats, lies, acts out violently. In none of these instances is play absent; it is in fact provocative. Here, play requires the partner's submission and omnipotence based on the interplay of colluding narcissisms, on the real desire to harm, debase, and destroy the other. I am sure everyone will understand to whom I refer.

Let me say that I think it is better to know what enemy you fight, rather than want to save him by showing that *you* have not been destroyed, or that the good-mother is still present.

During these last few years we have witnessed many examples of perverted playing, of dirty playing. Such play is not based on an interchange, but on the will to dominate; it is a way of imposing one's will, and the will to submit. It is a kind of play that is impregnated with destructiveness. I think Winnicott could not accept that destructiveness could also be transformed into a sort of play that brought not only a kind of enjoyment, but was also a way of feeding one's omnipotence.

To come back to the quotation, I also agree that psychoanalysis is a highly sophisticated phenomenon of the twentieth century. Yet, the psychoanalytic situation can be spoilt by different factors: the partners' inability to play, or their propensity to get stuck in repetitive compulsions, or, as we have seen recently, being used by the analyst to cure his own pathology—just as perverts pretend to cure others by convincing them to become perverts as well.

All these occurrences are also varieties of playing. Therefore ,we cannot consider playing as an aspect of health and all the other occurrences I have mentioned as non-playing. Just as we have dreams, we also have nightmares, nocturnal terrors, or somnambulism that, although being failures of dreams, are varieties of the psychic life of the sleeper just as much as are dreams.

In wanting to put play on the side of health, Winnicott also wanted to relate it to a satisfactory mother–infant relationship based on trust and developing into group relationships. According to my ideas, playing belongs to group as well as psychic phenomena—including dreaming, fantasizing, forging fictions, and myths. If I have to find a trait to define it, I shall have to turn not to a Winnicottian concept, but to a Bionian one. I would make the hypothesis that it could be one of the applications of Bion's "alpha" function. And just as Bion created the symbol "K" for Knowledge, he also created "−K" as its complement. I believe that play, apart from its emotional value, is a form of thought (like the dream) or of knowledge that, according to some patients, is a form of not knowing. In the same way, just as treacherous, cruel, and destructive plays are forms of non-playing, they can also be seen as negative playing. Nothing is left to chance. The winner or the loser (as in the negative therapeutic reaction) is known in advance. Domination infiltrates the whole playing. It is difficult to extract oneself from these "foul plays".

Why turn to this abstraction? Because, to me, the specificity of play is to change reality into something else, something that transforms what is unbearable in reality—be it internal or external. While I agree with Winnicott about the localization of play at the limit of internal and external reality, I am afraid that Winnicott again, and for the same reason, neglected to speak of the links that exist between reality and horror. It is difficult to accept that external reality is only objectively perceived. The distinction, of course, holds when compared to the omnipresence of subjectivity. The least we can say about external reality is that there is too much horror in it: wars, delinquency, natural catastrophes, epidemics, unemployment, terrorism. This is our daily world. I wonder how we could bear all the traumas inflicted by reality without play. And all these themes become favourite topics of play for children.

Let us consider further "playing and reality". The association was first made by Freud in his paper "Creative writers and daydreaming", where he writes:

> The child's best loved and most intense occupation is with his play or games. Might we not say that every child at play behaves like a creative writer in that he creates a world of his own, or, rather, rearranges the things of this world in a new way which pleases him. It would be wrong to think he does not take that world seriously; on the contrary, he takes his play very seriously and he invests a lot of emotion in it. The opposite of play is not what is serious but what is real. In spite of all the emotion with which he constructs his world of play, the child distinguishes it quite well from reality; and he likes to link his imagined objects and situations to the tangible and visible things of the real world. [Freud, 1908e, pp. 141–154]

This linking is all that differentiates the child's "play" from "fantasizing" (ibid., pp. 143–144). While Winnicott constantly repeats that he is not in disagreement with Freud but adds to his theory, on the topic of play there is not a single reference to Freud's work. He could have paid attention to Freud's even earlier remarks in "Psychopathic characters on the stage" (1942a), where he observes:

"Being present as an interested spectator at a spectacle or play [*schau-spiel* written in two words to underline the components of play] does for adults what play does for children" (*ibid.*, p. 30). Here we have the importance of witness, which will be taken up by Winnicott in a very different way. It is also surprising that we find no mention about the cotton-reel game, which was considered famous by so many writers, from Isaacs to Lacan. Nor do we find anything on the precise remark that Freud made in "Inhibitions, symptoms and anxiety" (1926d), stating that "through play the ego which has experienced a trauma passively repeats its activity in the play. Thus changing from passivity to activity, they attempt to master their experiences physically" (*ibid.*, p. 167).

I suppose that in this instance Winnicott did not care about Freud because what he had in mind was the Kleinian technique. He criticized Melanie Klein's conception of play, which considered the interpretation of the play only as an equivalent of fantasy (seen as a direct expression of the instinct) but neglected its study *per se*. To some extent Winnicott comes closer to Freud, for instance, when he emphasizes the near withdrawal state of the child playing as being akin to the concentration of older children and adults (Winnicott, 1971).

This concentration is also close to a sort of suspension of the relation to reality that can even be compared to a negative hallucination. It would be more appropriate to say a suspension of the belief in reality, a neglect of it, though it is not ignored, which looks like a splitting or denial of it. Returning to Winnicott's quotation that "psychoanalysis is the highly sophisticated twentieth century phenomenon", its source can be traced back to Winnicott's first psychoanalytic paper, "Primitive emotional development", in which he recalls his beginnings in psychoanalysis. Having decided that he had to study psychosis in analysis, he writes:

> I have had about a dozen psychic adult patients and half of them have rather extensively been analysed. This happened in the war and I might say that I hardly noticed the Blitz, being all the time engaged in analysis of psychotic patients who are notoriously and maddeningly oblivious of bombs, earth-quakes and floods. [Winnicott, 1945]

So, if the psychotic denies and represses reality, the analyst, in the sophisticated play that he plays with them, has to share some of this denial—not to the point of behaving like them, but by adopting an attitude which suspends his relationship to reality.

This is true of all play, because this attitude is a prerequisite in order to foster that mode of functioning, already described by Freud in children's play, where the child creates a new world or rearranges his perceptions and combines different elements in conformity with his will, building a new order.

Freud himself, in his paper "The loss of reality in neurosis and psychosis" (1924e), thus compares the delusional world of the psychotic to the world of fantasy:

> It can hardly be doubted that the world of fantasy plays the same part, in psychosis, as in neurosis and that here too it is the store house from which the materials or the pattern for building the new reality [the delusion] are derived. But whereas the new imaginary external world of psychosis attempts to put itself in the place of external reality, that of neurosis on the contrary is apt *like the play of children* [my italics] to attach itself to a piece of reality—a different piece from the one it has to defend itself and to lend that piece a special importance and a secret meaning which we (not always quite appropriately) call a *symbolic* one. Thus we see that both in psychosis and neurosis there comes into consideration the question not only of *loss of reality* but also of a substitute for reality. [Freud, 1924e, p. 187]

Two remarks have to be observed here. The first is that, according to Freud, play is not only related to health but can develop in many directions: one is the creative writing of fiction, the other is neurosis and, by extension (if we think of psychosis), delusion.

The fantasy of the psychotic is not only a substitute of play, as in neurosis, but also pretends *to be* reality, more appropriately called a new reality. It is no longer a question of play, but of a substitute for the lost reality. When considering borderline cases, it is sometimes difficult to trace the frontier between the playing of the neurotic and the replacement of reality of the psychotic. My feeling is that the dimension of playing, even when the patient is akin to psychosis, is never absent—because the belief in the new reality is never complete and it can be subject to criticism in the oscillation to and from the psychotic pole.

It is true that the great majority of the meanings attached to play are positive, but we cannot forget that play is also associated with cheating, from which it is inseparable: to play into somebody's hands, to be caught in someone else's play, or to be trapped. I think that all these expressions can be seen as perversions of play. This confirms my idea that playing is a category beyond good or bad.

The second remark to be observed is Freud's conclusion on the loss of reality in neurosis and psychosis. What appears important to me is the couple: *loss* of reality, and the *substitute* for reality. In play, the loss element is minimal and the substitution element maximal. In illness, be it neurosis or psychosis, the element of loss predominates and the element of substitution is subordinate to it.

Loss and substitution go together; whenever we think of one we should also think of the other. When play is performed, there is loss behind it. It is not by chance that Winnicott's examples deal mostly with the kind of separations that cannot be overcome, or can be only apparently overcome. When we think of loss, let us remember Freud's phrase: "But it is evident that a precondition for the setting up of reality, is that the objects have been lost which once brought real satisfaction" (1924e, p. 236). What is the compensation for the price paid for this setting-up?

During examination we find in many, many cases that in the child's background, whether in the present or in the past, there is a *depressed mother*. Here we have an example of a double loss, or even of a reflected one: the loss represented by the mother's depression, and also the effect produced on the child who also loses something although he does not know exactly what. I have treated the subject rather extensively in my essay, "The dead mother" (1999), but this evening I want to concentrate on the double-sided loss and the reflective effect that the mother's depression has on the child.

In *Playing and Reality* (1971) Winnicott gives several examples and I shall select some of them, remarkable to me, which are very representative. He begins the first chapter, "Transitional objects and transitional phenomena", with a section entitled "String"—which he had already published in *Child Psychology and Psychiatry* (1961) and also in *The Maturational Processes and the Facilitating Environment* (1965). This clinical case is meaningful to him. He wants to show how a child copes with separations and loss, using the case of a seven-year-old boy of normal intelligence. I do not want here to give a detailed account of Winnicott's consultations (the clinical depression of the mother, her successive hospitalizations, her attention being turned away from the boy when his sister was born, etc.), but instead to concentrate on the "Squiggle" game that the boy accepted very easily without giving an abnormal impression of himself. Winnicott writes: "The boy's laziness immediately became evident and also nearly everything I did was translated by him into something associated with string" (1971). After the interview with the boy, the parents confirmed his obsessive preoccupations with a piece of string, which they had not mentioned before.

Winnicott tries to open up the situation by explaining to the mother her boy's fear of separation from his mother. She is, of course, sceptical. Six months later, she is convinced that it is true. Considering other details about the lack of contact between the mother and the boy, Winnicott concludes that the string is used as a *denial of separation*, rather than as a technique of communication— "becoming a thing in itself", an expression reminiscent of Bion that we do not find anywhere else in Winnicott. In a note added in 1969, Winnicott sadly came to the conclusion that "this boy could not be cured of his illness".

There were no significant changes from the first time Winnicott saw the boy at seven, and ten years later. The boy could not be kept from running back to his home from wherever he was placed. In adolescence he became addicted to drugs and played with a rope, hanging himself upside-down (perhaps symbolizing the murdering of time). Nobody dared call his toys "toys". I see this case as a chronic repetitive compulsion—maybe related to separation anxiety marked by its denial, but also characterized in Freudian terms as a predominance of loss and no possibility of substituting for reality. Playing is very restricted and its creative power is limited to producing icons of separations.

Two other examples are also illustrative of Winnicott's ideas. In the chapter "Playing: a theoretical statement", Winnicott describes the case of Edmund, aged two and a half, and Diana, aged five. In both cases the children were not the object of the consultations, but came along with their mothers. Winnicott had to accept them. Each of these consultations turned into double consultations, with Winnicott listening to the mother and still keeping an eye on the children. Edmund very quickly asks, after a few minutes: "Where are the toys?" That was the only thing he said throughout the hour. While Winnicott was talking with the mother, Edmund started to play, putting small train parts on the table, joining them up. Soon, though he was only two feet apart from the mother, he came back to her and got on to her lap. After about twenty minutes he began to liven up, getting a fresh supply of toys. The mother explained that her boy needed contact with her breast as well as with her lap. At one point, when he was trying to keep some distance from the mother, he started stammering. As a baby he would refuse everything except the breast, even the bottle. His attention was then caught by one end of a piece of string. Sometimes he would make a gesture resembling the plugging in of the end of the string, as though it were an electric flex, to his mother's thigh. To make a long story short, the important thing is Winnicott's awareness that the boy's play was illustrative of what the mother was talking about, although it was she who was talking to Winnicott. He writes: "As it happened, I was mirroring what was taking place and giving it a quality of communication." This mirroring situation seemed to him to be fundamental.

In this case we can observe the boy's apparent indifference about what was happening between the mother and Winnicott. Edmund did not seem to be interested or to care. The reality of the situation was not denied, hidden by some sort of screen. But this situation at first escaped the observer—who appeared blind. Only Winnicott managed to understand that the boy's play was another dramatized and displaced version of what the mother was talking about. If we consider the couple loss and substitution, we see that substitution completely covers the threatening of loss by disguising it in the child's play. The mirroring situation was not only Winnicott's understanding, but also the child's playing activity mirroring the relationship between the mother's narration and her listener. Play here is the result of an attempt at transformation and manages to cheat any observer other than Winnicott or any other psychoanalyst. We are not here in a situation of rigid repetitive compulsion but in a trajectory that goes to and fro between the mother and Edmund. We can see that, far from realizing where he stands, he seems himself to be lost. While wanting to be with his mother, he tries, unsuccessfully, to escape her. As Winnicott says: "the boy communicates an ebb of movement in him away from, and back to, dependence" (Winnicott, 1971). We can define this play as the impossibility of abandoning reduplication with an attempt to become distant from the object. On the whole, the mother responded adequately.

But the most interesting example is Diana. One cannot forget, of course, that she is five years old and in any case has a more complex psychic organization than Edmund.

As in the previous case, Winnicott had to conduct two consultations in parallel: one with the mother, who is there for herself, being in distress, and simultaneously a "play relationship" with the daughter, Diana. Winnicott accomplishes a threefold task: he has to give full attention to the mother, play with the child, and record the nature of Diana's play so as to write his paper. Diana presents herself at the front door, putting forward a teddy bear. Here, we see the play preceding the consultation: Diana is using the teddy bear as a representative of herself. This is probably why Winnicott, before starting the consultation or even looking at the mother, addresses Diana; first he asks her the name of the teddy bear. "Just Teddy," she replies. We shall see the multiple identity of Teddy: he can stand as a representative of Diana, or as her ill brother, or as Diana's imaginary child. After a while, probably feeling overwhelmed and unable to give the mother the attention she needs, Winnicott suddenly puts his ear to the teddy bear (using the transitional object in order to enable the situation to change and move into some other space) and says to Diana: "I heard him say something. I think he wants someone to play with". Thus, he does not leave the child alone, but enhances an imaginary relationship. He tells the child about a woolly lamb that she would find at the other end of the room. Acting in this way, Winnicott stimulates her maternal identification. Then Diana puts the teddy bear and the lamb (which was considerably bigger than the bear) together; here Winnicott confesses that perhaps his suggestion was in the hope of getting the bear out of his jacket—Diana had stuffed it in his breast-pocket, curious to see how far it would go down. Her play therefore alluded to her brother's birth and Winnicott's response, calling the lamb to join in the play, was perfectly logical, though, I believe, unconscious. Diana decided that teddy and the lamb were her children. She emphasized the fact that they were not twins: the lamb was to be born first and only then the teddy. After the "birth" was finished, she put the newly-born baby in a bed she had improvised, placing each of them at separate ends in order to prevent them from meeting in the middle and fighting under the bedclothes. After a while, she placed them peacefully at the top of the bed. She then fetched a lot of toys and played with them. Winnicott's précis of this is: "The playing was orderly and there were several different themes that developed, each one kept separate from the other". Winnicott joins in the girl's play spontaneously and exclaims: "Oh! Look! You are putting on the floor around the babies' heads the dreams that they are having while they are asleep!" (Winnicott, 1971).

The child, intrigued by the idea, was developing various themes as if dreaming the dream for the babies. This shift of emphasis allows Winnicott to come back to the mother, who cries about her other child's cardiac illness. (Diana says: "He has a hole in his heart.") Winnicott comments on the mother's crying about her ill son. The communication being direct and factual, Diana is reassured.

I shall now pause to make some observations on these examples chosen by Winnicott. Both children show not only a capacity to be alone in the presence of the mother, but also in the presence of a mother talking to a third person whom she wants to see—not about themselves, but because of her own distress. In one case we see how difficult it is for the child to be separated from the mother, but what seems important to me is Winnicott's awareness that the child's play reproduces in action what the mother and himself were talking about, even when that was about the child himself. With Edmund there is an unconscious will to reproduce and transform what is perceived from reality, even in a limited way. Nevertheless, play appears as a development of the relation to reality and a rebuilding of a transposed and created reality. But in Diana's case, the play constantly increases its meaning, extends its connection, and becomes more complex by including a potential dream that is largely the same as the play but in a disguised way.

In the second case, i.e. with Diana, play is not only a reaction of something happening in reality but is a creation in itself, involving first a transitional object (the teddy bear) that she has to introduce into Winnicott's pocket as if he were pregnant—just like the mother when she was expecting the ill child. There is a concern of how far the teddy bear can go down (perhaps being aborted or falling through a hole?). A polysemous fantasy develops wherein the two animals are exposed to fight in the middle of the bed under the clothes. This symbolism is probably a shift to the parents' primal scene, then sleeping quietly. But the most amazing thing is Winnicott's interpretation of the toys that Diana puts at the end of the imaginary bed: i.e., that they represent the dreams that the transitional objects have while they are asleep. To me this is an essential step forward, because reflection is no longer limited to reproduce more or less in disguise what is taking place in reality, as with Edmund, but demonstrates to a certain degree how play can represent a dream of which we know nothing, which is created by the transitional objects themselves. It is a movement of inwardness as deep as a dream, apparently incoherent, made of shreds and patches, a product of the rearrangement of both elements of internal and external reality. Play is a manifestation of the mind that I understand as being the result of undoing the pieces belonging to reality, in order to recombine them and create a potential existence.

What I am attempting to say is that it is not enough to interpret the content of the play; we have to understand its structure. Perhaps am I not fully satisfied with a definition of play in terms of transitional phenomena, or standing between internal and external reality, symbolizing a potential space of a reunion between the mother and the baby at the place and time where separation took place. What I need to understand is how perceptions and fantasies are the reproductions of an experience both internal and external and, even more, to be able to perceive in play the extension of the mirroring relationship, its dynamics in a system more or less open to new developments, and the reflection inside the play through which we may understand the interconnected fantasies as well as their possibility of being transposed in another unconscious structure—as the formation of a dream.

In a few words, playing, fantasizing, creating fictions, telling tales, and even imagining the dreams that appear in the play, belong to one and the same world. Its interpretation is bound to the complexity of the inter-connexion and the transformation of communication through meaning accompanied by the changing identity of the addressees. Compared to other structures marked by primary processes such as dreams, fantasies, and so on, I suggest that playing differs from them because it is three-dimensional, not because it has depth but because it looks like reality.

One element not to be forgotten is that even when the child plays alone, there is always someone watching or, as in the situation we described, someone talking to someone else about what is going on. It may be difficult for the analyst to know where he stands in this situation. Instead of thinking that he is systematically in the place of the mother, he may also be in the place of the person to whom the mother is speaking. It is important never to forget the place of the analytic third, and also always to remember that between the play and the person (adult–child), there is always an invisible screen that forbids too direct interpretations. Just as free association is essential to analytic work, play has to be considered as a creation of free association processes.

It is not quite clear to me why Winnicott gave the chapter following "Playing: a theoretical statement"—which is so accomplished and gives the feeling that he perfectly understood and had definitely dealt with the subject—the title of "Playing: a creative activity, and the search of the self"; it is so different from the preceding one.

I believe that Winnicott was here tackling the problem of the pre-condition of play. Winnicott says that only in playing is communication possible and the individual able to be creative. Creative experiences are sometimes the only possible way for the individual to be himself. Creativity is not a specialized activity but a feature of life and total living.

What is important in this perspective is to react on non-purposive state, a condition close to the supposed unintegrated state of the beginning of life to which one has to come back. The search of the self has to go back to formlessness. Non-purposive being, formless mind activity, are free from anxiety and defence. These are conditions favourable for a search of the self. It is difficult not to think about free association as a first step towards this aim. Winnicott gives an illustration of a case that he has seen in a very long session (the patient needed a session of indefinite length, once a week, after having had treatment five times a week). Tolerance of chaos during the session may lead at the end to a finding of the lost self. There is not a single element of play in the paper. There are, instead, lots of destructive thoughts related to others or about herself, lots of catastrophic fantasies, the feeling of never being oneself, memories of feeling empty. After an hour and a half, the patient feels: "Just drifting like the clouds", and then the negative feelings return with the impression of having spoilt her life and not really being in the session. When finally Winnicott has the impression that the patient is in the session, he gives this interpretation to her: "All sorts of things happen and they wither. This is the myriad deaths you have died. But if someone is there, someone who can give you back what happened, then the details dealt with in this way become part of you, and do not die" (Winnicott, 1971).

Though the interpretation demonstrates Winnicott's creativity more than the patient's, he also introduces a very important idea: however bad or negative are the experiences, the presence of some-one just watching, acting as a mirror, gives to the scattered part a unity that is reflected to the patient and becomes part of him. We have some evidence of Winnicott's intuition being right when the patient confesses later in the session "that she made use in her room of a lot of mirrors for some person to reflect back. But there is no one".

This is exactly what Winnicott does for her; in taking notes, writing interpretations he will never tell, being present, waiting for the time when she will be able to be herself, Winnicott is the mirror who reflects something other than the negative hallucination that the patient has of her own image.

But we now come to a general conclusion, as Winnicott beautifully formulates to the patient: "*It was yourself you were searching*" (1971). The patient responded after a while: "Yes, I see one could postulate the existence of a Me from the question as from the searching." This to me sounds unexpectedly very Cartesian. The theoretical statement closes the chapter:

> The searching can come only from desultory formless functioning or perhaps from rudimentary playing, as if in a neutral zone. It is only here in this unintegrated state of the personality, that which we call creative, can appear. This, if reflected back, *but only if reflected back*, becomes part of the organised individual personality and eventually this in summation makes the individual to be to be found and eventually enable himself or herself to postulate the existence of the self. [Winnicott, 1971]

I have some doubt that Winnicott really wanted to be found, as he explained that the true self is hidden, secret and mute; maybe it is in speculation of the formlessness or in elementary play.

There is no play without reflection. Even when the child plays alone, someone in his mind is looking at his play, someone who maybe understands the play that he himself does not understand. From that chapter on we shall see that most of the other chapters will include a reference to reflection. With regard to the distorted reflection to which Winnicott alludes in his famous interpretation to a male patient who had to deny and keep as far as possible from consciousness the non-masculine element of his personality, we note that Winnicott says to him: "I am listening to a girl, I know perfectly well that you are a man, but I am listening to a girl and I am talking to a girl. I am telling this girl: 'You are talking about penis envy' " (Winnicott, 1971).

Winnicott makes it clear in his interpretation, which has been compared to playing, that it was hearing that was like a representative of the mother's look: "This madness of mine enabled him to see himself as a girl *from my position*" (*ibid.*). This is a good example of a distorting mirror.

In some other chapters we again encounter the importance of reflection, as in "Mirror rôle of mother and family in child development". We see, therefore, that it is not enough to compare psychotherapy with the overlap of two curtains: a third element must come into play—and this is their potential mutual reflection.

If we now turn towards the theory and the area of illusion between the mother (breast) and the infant, we also imply an element of reflection. Maybe the origin of this reflectivity is to be found in Winnicott's thinking, in an unfinished book. The intermediary area does not exist from the start. It is an attempt to reunify what has been separated at the place and time of separation. Of this occasion, Winnicott says something so bold that he is afraid of spelling it out: "The intermediary stage is referred to as a layer of the mind constituted of an aspect of the mother and an aspect of the baby, both being mixed in one" (Winnicott, 1971).

This for me involves some kind of inner reflection between the two parts that the infant will try to find again in the intermediary area. I suspect this to be related to the topic of transference. In the cases quoted of Edmund and Diana, we have seen how reflection is imprisoned in the first one, and open in the second. This hypothesis also applies to the delocalization of cultural experience. The value of Winnicott's thesis is the interrelation between the intermediate area of transitional phenomena, its location between internal and external reality, and its connection with symbolization.

When we speak of cultural experience, play comes to the fore in certain privileged domains. To play, is to act. It is difficult for me not to conclude by speaking about theatre, because there is in the theatre a special occurrence that is worth thinking about. We all know the existence in some plays of play within the play: *Hamlet* and *The Tempest* easily come to mind, but to me the most astonishing example is *A Midsummer Night's Dream*. Let us understand that reflection is not enough; what we need in order to understand the mind is the reflection of reflection—as in the playing within *A Midsummer Night's Dream*. When we can arrive at a point of sophistication where a player can say, playing his part in the play that is within the play:

> In this same interlude it doth befall
> That I—one Snout by name—present a wall.
> And such a wall as I would have you think
> That had in it a crannied hole or chink,
> Through which the lovers, Pyramus and Thisbe,
> Did whisper often, very secretly.
> This loam, this roughcast, and this stone doth show
> That I am that same wall; the truth is so.

The mirror becomes a wall represented by a man with a hole through which we whisper, often very secretly, with our patients. The truth is so.

References

Freud, S. (1908e). *S.E.*, *IX*: 141–154. London: Hogarth.

Freud, S. (1924e). The loss of reality in neurosis and psychosis. *S.E.*, *XIX*: London: Hogarth.

Freud, S. (1926d). *S.E.*, *XX*: 167. London: Hogarth.

Freud, S. (1942a)[1905–06]. *S.E.*, *VII*: 30. London: Hogarth.

Green, A. (1999). *The Dead Mother: The Work of André Green*. London: Routledge.

Winnicott, D. W. (1945). Primitive emotional development. *International Journal of Psycho-Analysis, 26.*

Winnicott, D. W. (1971), *Playing and Reality.* London: Tavistock.

Winnicott, D. W. (1988). *Human Nature,* C. Bollas, M. Davis, & R. Shepherd (Eds.). London: Free Association Books.

Vote of thanks

Cesare Sacerdoti

O n behalf of us all I would like to thank Professor Green for a fascinating lecture.

As always, André has been provocative. There is a tendency to canonize many authors—but certainly that is not what André ever does; he always urges us primarily to read, and then to read again. He teaches us that just because something has not been looked at, does not mean that it is not *worth* looking at. That, basically, is the message that I have received from him tonight: it is no use repeating nice little packages and saying we need take just these, and then off we go. André has challenged all of us here tonight; some of us did not like it, that is quite obvious, but frankly I for one did not expect anything else! But this is success. This is tonight's value.

When André speaks to people, he invariably asks if they have actually read the paper, idea, or book that was being considered. Too many of us tend to read between the lines—and not the lines themselves. It happens far, far too often.

I am sure that even those of you who are not perhaps as pleased as you expected to be with the lecture, who have not been "massaged" in a nice way but have, rather, been stimulated—and even perhaps pricked a little—will nevertheless join me in thanking Professor André Green for his masterly exposition of some most recondite concepts that are not perhaps noticed in the way that they should be, and not noticed often enough. Thank you very much.

Addendum to lecture

André Green

*Conjectures about Winnicott's unconscious
counter-transference in the case of Masud Khan, in the
light of the Wynne Godley case*

I n February 2001 Wynne Godley published a paper, "Saving
Masud Khan" (2001), which created a great deal of concern
among the analysts of the British Psychoanalytical Society, but
not only among them. It generated much discussion and brought
more plainly into the open the question of boundary violations. The
Society's Ethics Committee, represented by A.-M. Sandler, replied
officially to Godley, addressing many of his complaints (2004).
Exceptionally, although not uniquely, prior to this particular inci-
dent, other papers had dealt with the Masud Khan case—mostly by
Linda Hopkins, who is currently working on a biography of him.
In one of her papers, published before Godley's paper appeared,
she deals specifically with Winnicott's analysis of Masud Khan
(1998).

This Addendum proposes to show how Winnicott's unconscious
counter-transference was a contributory factor in the failure of the
treatment. Its failure was also the result of some of Winnicott's

debatable ideas on technique, which have their own blind spots. All of this, combined, offered little hope—if there was any to begin with—of saving Masud Khan. Furthermore, it seeks to illustrate not only how play can transgress the limits of the setting but how it can also be turned into "foul play" (as in *Hamlet*). Linda Hopkins has dealt in her paper with Masud Khan's application of play techniques to analytic consultation and the treatment of adults (Hopkins, 2000); here, however, we venture beyond what she reports.

Before continuing my discussion, I would inform the reader that I had a long acquaintance with Masud Khan and that it ended on unfriendly terms. That has no connection with the present matter. I also personally met Wynne Godley on three occasions: the first time was long before the publication of his article, and at the time I was not even aware that he had been in analysis; the subsequent encounters occurred after I had read it. I must stress that nothing in the piece that follows has been drawn from my relations with either Masud Khan or Wynne Godley.

My principal sources are Godley's article (2001), Rodman's biography on Winnicott (2003) and, to a lesser extent, Linda Hopkins' papers before 2001. These have been used to provide an analytic *après coup* interpretation of the events in order to try to explain what may have happened, over and beyond Godley's description. Finally, I would add that Wynne Godley, in my strongest opinion, is not the kind of patient to leave any doubt about his complaints.

In the beginning of his paper Wynne Godley describes concisely what he terms "his state of dissociation". His self-observation, in few words, is convincing. He describes his false self as being split from the body. He tells of living in a waking dream, of his paradoxical insensitivity, of his sense of estrangement when faced with unpredicted situations, of his panic attacks, delusional beliefs, etc.

All of this fits in remarkably with Winnicott's clinical descriptions, which do not belong to the range of neurotic disorders. We can therefore imagine that Winnicott was quite familiar with this type of pathology when he referred the case to Masud Khan. It has been suggested, though this is open to question, that Anna Freud was asked for her approval—Godley having married Kathleen Garman Epstein, Lucian Freud's first wife.

I shall not describe the accumulation of traumas in Godley's case history as the reader may refer to them direct elsewhere. What

I wish to focus upon is a maternal relationship on the one hand, involving a careless, neglectful, over-seductive mother (she used to walk about naked in front of the child, creating an erotic intimacy with him, and confess to him her sexual pleasure with men) and on the other, a paternal relationship involving an impotent (supposedly), humiliating, cruel, shallow, invalid, and severely alcoholic father. This family situation caused to develop in the child not only a huge narcissistic retreat and organization but also a feminine identification mixed with denial of the mother's carelessness.

In spite of his mother's mismanagement the boy, fascinated as he was by her seductive manoeuvres, did not complain about her. Towards the father, however, one suspects a strong hatred due to his ineffectiveness. I would suggest that the child blamed him for his inability to offer any grounds for a masculine identification.

It is generally known how Winnicott underestimated the importance of the father and of sexuality, and denied their fundamental role in the shaping of the personality. For instance, no one—neither Winnicott nor Khan—seemed to pay any attention to the fact that at seventeen Godley confessed to ignoring the existence of the vagina, and to not knowing that men ejaculate. These are far from ordinary sexual symptoms: a kind of split in the body amounting to an amputation of sexuality. It would be unreasonable to think that these symptoms could be cured automatically after caring about the self, whether you call it artificial or false. These facts may be related to Godley's confession of the skill he acquired during childhood that he described as "a spectacular ability to *not* see, identify or shrewdly evaluate people and situations". I believe that this, which I connect with negative hallucination, always means that one looks for similar character traits towards the significant people of one's environment. This is what happened in Godley's so-called analysis between analyst and consultant analyst.

With such a disturbed background one would expect many occurrences of symptoms along with different sorts of fixations. Wynne Godley, despite having many reasons to be angry with his mother, apparently did not hate her. He seems also to have liked his stepmother (who eventually committed suicide). Indeed, it is not stated anywhere that he had difficult relationships with other women. He seemed to have realized at some time during the analysis, and as a kind of revelation: "My father hated me". There is no evidence that his father brutalized or ill-treated him. One might, of course, relate that hatred to the projection of the son experiencing excessively erotic, too-close intimacy with his mother, whom he visited at her home (his parents having been separated from his birth). I am not saying that one should understand this as a manifestation of an Oedipus complex, for that was not structured at the time.

In any event, neither Winnicott nor Khan seem to have paid attention to that central fact: the hatred of the father. It is my assumption that Godley came to realize that his father's inconsistent behaviour, with its heavy alcoholism, was an unconscious way of attacking the father image. It was, furthermore, to induce contempt; above all, it was to remove any possibility of a positive identification in manhood. A sort of hallucinatory vision involving his father had accompanied this: "Unless he justifies himself I must save him", thus witnessing a role-reversal in the parent–child relationship, a splitting of the hate, a reparation process and, as it were, a secret oath: "I must save him" (meaning, in truth, "I must sacrifice myself").

Godley seems to have been quite aware of this when he chose the title for his paper. There was, however, no reference as to how it had been interpreted. What I am implying is that, consciously or unconsciously, Khan did everything that was possible to confirm Godley's secret promise by repeating the father's behaviour (being also an awful drunkard), by multiplying boundary violations, by trying to impress his patient with his important relations, by interfering with his marital relationship, by telling him about his own marriage with a famous dancer, by being scornful and projective, by keeping him at a distance, by giving savage interpretations about the supposed (?) wish of the patient to be cuddled by him, etc., etc.,—but also by repeating the behaviour of the promiscuous mother. Because Godley remained unimpressed, Khan felt he had to double the dose: associating the patient and his wife with his own social life. During a party, he is said to have declared to an elegant woman attending: "He and I the same, Aristocrats." This is a key phrase. Khan was playing sameness although he always felt the British regarded him as an inferior, a native. In fact, there could be no equality in the relationship since systematically Khan was obsessed with dominating his patient, humiliating him, and continuously boasting about his own exploits.

Khan had made a serious mistake in underlining the aristocratic background of patient and analyst. As for Godley, the son of a Lord who thought himself so noble that nobody would notice he had been drinking, it was easy to see that the condition was a painful one. The presence of the father was that of a shadow, the son seeing him as an invalid and very different from ordinary fathers. Khan never lost an opportunity to draw attention to his own powerful father, who had made him his sole heir even though he had seven other children. On the other hand, he rarely mentioned his father's marriage to a woman sometimes referred to as a courtesan but who may have been a dancer; Khan's mother had been a drug addict and had given birth to an illegitimate child just before Khan. The comparison with Godley's family situation is striking: an impotent father married to a woman who proclaimed her right to promiscuity. One might imagine that not only did Khan idealize his father—which he denied—but also, as suggested by his violence (like that of Godley's father), that the father image was less prestigious and more terrorized than the one presented by the son. Both Godley's father and Khan made very expensive gifts to Godley—as if asking the son for forgiveness.

Now what about Winnicott in all this? Winnicott's own father, although mayor of Plymouth and respected in the city, was always considered a member of the lower middle class. Winnicott could not identify in the least with the son of a worthy burgher. (Here perhaps we may remind ourselves that Winnicott, though divorced from his first wife and involved in a longstanding relationship, nevertheless had to await his father's death before remarrying.) It seems that Khan's ostentatiously provocative behaviour (involving the "jet-set" society) was a kind of Don Juanistic accumulation of sinful acts to provoke the wrath of the Lord (his own). Winnicott, however, instead of interpreting Khan's wish to be punished by him, kept silent—"*Qui ne dit mot consent*"; he even indulged in telephone calls during Godley's sessions in which erotic jokes were exchanged that the patient could perfectly well overhear. Winnicott would not at any cost adopt a prohibitive attitude towards Khan until certain limits were exceeded. What we do know is that Khan was infuriated by Winnicott's passivity; Winnicott concentrated all his hopes on the virtue of "holding".

I believe that Khan tried to seduce Winnicott by his boundary violations (Rodman, 2003), just as he had seduced his own father.

But Winnicott's nature—"too nice", as he qualified himself— ˙˙
certainly rendered him incapable of being an authoritarian figure.
Nothing is more revealing than Khan's own words at Winnicott's
memorial meeting: "Some of us—and I am one of those—think he
let the side down by his special stance of humility, which is larger
than arrogance and authority."

So. Winnicott sought to resist Khan's provocation. Did
Winnicott realize that his obstinacy had inflicted a narcissistic blow
on Khan, who felt humiliated by the modesty of his analyst, a bril-
liant mind who could have become "the King of Analysts" to the
Prince that he pretended to be? Winnicott also humiliated Khan by
limiting his power of seduction. Performing editorial work after his
analysis on Sunday mornings, Khan even boasted of "having edited
much of Winnicott's output in the last twenty years of his life"
(Rodman, 2003). Joyce Coles, Winnicott's secretary, expressed
doubts about this. Yet he was never invited to lunch and Winnicott's second wife, Clare, was fiercely opposed to giving him access
to the privacy of the Winnicotts' home. After Winnicott's death she
also declined Khan's request to become her husband's literary
executor. She gave him nothing. This further increased Khan's
hostility to women and his inability to get the better of them (quite
unlike his boasts about men), coupled with the disappointing real-
ization that Winnicott preferred his wife to him. Not being made
Winnicott's literary heir was a traumatic blow. Khan tried to take
revenge on Godley by endeavouring to break up his marriage; he
introduced him to another woman and suggested that she, who
already had a child by another man (just like Khan's own mother),
would be a more suitable partner for him. Khan also secretly
invited Godley's wife to an interview with him. Ironically, at one
time, Khan's wife was in such a bad way that Winnicott asked Khan
to yield up his sessions to her!

It is plausible to claim that Khan made every effort to ruin
Godley's marriage by suggesting another partner whom he could
totally control. The alternative partner was one of his analysands.
In fact, Khan wanted to succeed where he had failed with Winnicott—for he hated Winnicott's wife—by breaking the husband–
wife relationship. Time and again Winnicott's wife showed great
pride in her success of making her husband potent, thus infuriating ˙˙
Khan.

I presume that when Khan abruptly decided to interrupt his fifteen years of analysis, it was because he had been discussing with Winnicott the above-mentioned literary execution with the aim of obtaining from Winnicott some form of official approval. He failed to do so because of Clare's strong opposition.

We cannot charge Winnicott with being mistaken and seduced by Khan, nor of his having taken pleasure in Khan's arrogant behaviour, which Winnicott himself could not afford. I would say that Winnicott's focus on primary emotional development, disbelief in sexuality, and his very late discovery of the role of the father, together led him to give up on any analysis of Masud Khan's homosexuality and masochism. Winnicott would not believe that these could be responsible for his pathology, just as he did not believe in interpretations. I would like to add that the choice is not between not interpreting and interpreting in the Kleinian way. In any event, to believe that a "holding" relationship has the capacity to overcome these psychopathic behaviours is more than optimistic; but, by all accounts, that belief maintained a mutually seductive relationship—a major error.

Was Masud Khan analysable? I guess many analysts today would say that he was not. I do not blame Winnicott for his mistakes, but I do regret his being blind to that part of psychoanalytic theory that was too close to his own pathology (being too nice, or being devilish). The result is not only our concern at boundary violations—though this would deserve another paper—but also on the sexualization of post-transference relationships.

What is tragic in the intertwined histories and misfortunes of Godley, Khan, and Winnicott is that psychoanalysis has been the occasion of a sinister farce, of fateful repetitions, where compulsions belonging to one individual's history are transferred on to another in the wrong way, from analyst to patient when it should be the reverse—thereby alienating the individual from his own unconscious, without any real analysis.

Aside from all the mismanagements within the case, one thing strikes me in particular: it seems as if Godley's traumatic background induced a narcissistic structure that Khan, despite his acuteness, did not know how to handle. Wounded by his own therapeutic failure, Khan had the mad idea of trying to cure Godley's "artificial" self, i.e., pseudo narcissistic, by projecting his own "princely" narcissism on to Godley in the hope that it would change his into a more committed one. He did not succeed in his method—founded on shared "aristocracy". Instead, Khan became more and more furious, grew ever more dangerously psychopathic. Above all, he felt his grandiose self was wounded. Having transgressed all boundaries, Winnicott could no longer remain a "good enough" mother who cures everything, and he paid heavily for his mistake. He never showed his patients that he wished to embody the paternal law. Winnicott's remark about the case, having cut short the relationship between Godley and Khan, is interesting; he refers, as if in disgust, to: "all that social stuff".

Homosexuality is not only a sexual perversion; it may also be found in paranoia. It is a disguised way of castrating the father, stealing and destroying the father's penis because of envy. It is a subtle, indirect way of dominating the envied father figure who is also debased by the son's behaviour. Moreover, it is a way to take destructive revenge on the woman to whom the son is finally preferred: through the cheating, the lying (and even the stealing). Winnicott, however, did not take into consideration this aspect of Freudian theory.

In Shakespeare, Prince Hal, after his father's death, becomes the worthy and virtuous King Henry V. "Prince" Khan could never achieve this transformation because he never had access to the crown, the one crown he really envied and which is only obtained through writing. Masud Khan's papers were well received when they first appeared. Winnicott himself praised them. He even backed Khan when he applied to the British Society, ignoring the normal rule of neutrality. Moreover, Winnicott's support led him to believe that his seduction game had worked and that he would once more be made the unique heir! But it was doomed to failure. Today, few, if any, refer to Khan's work, whereas Winnicott's continues to be quoted, analysed and discussed. One might say, in spite of the "sound and fury", oblivion has had the better of Masud Khan—in all but the scandal.

I have tried to show the existence of a perversion of play in Masud Khan's treatment of Wynne Godley. But it was not only present in the Godley case. Indeed, in Masud Khan's papers he reveals how he engaged in games of backgammon with some of his patients, thereby misusing them also. He tells about another patient who had arrived at his session accompanied by his dog that frightened Khan. In the next session he hid behind the door of his consulting-room and waited until the unwary patient entered, before jumping on him and making barking noises at him like a wild dog. He explained the lesson to his patient: "This is to show you how one can feel when you come into the consulting-room with your hound." In Wynne Godley's case, however, the complicity of others helped subtly to pervert the whole thing into a social entertainment. Svetlana Beriosova, Khan's wife, was treated at the same time as her husband by Winnicott and was also conferred with during some of his regular sessions. Not surprisingly, she developed a deep scepticism about psychoanalysis.

How can we explain Winnicott's refusal, in the counter-transference process, to become a re-enactment of the paternal figure? Winnicott's own father played a significant role when he repaired a doll belonging to Winnicott's sister that Winnicott had badly damaged. Perhaps his father should be thanked for this act, but on the whole he remained distant towards his only son. He would refer all his son's existential questions to the Bible, saying that he would find the answers he looked for there. But in so doing, he refused to assume a fundamental paternal responsibility: that of being a model of masculine identification for his son. Most of the time Winnicott was left in the company of his mother and sisters.

On reading the descriptions of Winnicott's parents in Rodman's biography I cannot help believing that his mother—allowing for the possible limitations of a woman of her generation and character— was less involved than his father in the genesis of the false self in Winnicott's personal experience. His father, it appears to me, was more evocative of a "false self": more concerned and preoccupied with his own social position than with his son's difficulty in developing into a man. One example is his decision to send Winnicott off to boarding-school for having pronounced rude words. Although he was rather shallow, his son seemed to have feared him.

Ultimately, Masud Kahn's provocations were to prove fruitless, since no father figure emerged. Certainly, Winnicott admired Khan's skills and it is probable that his antisocial behaviour secretly attracted him. However, it was a long time before Winnicott discovered the importance of the father in accomplishing the process of separation between mother and child. Indeed, this understanding was to come at the end of his life: too late to save Masud Kahn. Winnicott had his first heart attack the same day his father died and his heart succumbed totally a few years later. He died enlightened but without ever having felt what it was to be a father. As for Khan, he felt orphaned by Winnicott's death: abandoned and left alone to struggle with his own self-destructive impulses. Nor could he expect help from anyone any more, having disappointed even the best of his friends. Anna Freud, to whom he went subsequently, was incapable of embodying the paternal figure—unlike potentially her father—that he so craved. In one of his rages Khan said to Godley: "You are a very tiresome and disappointing man." Did he likewise wish to be scourged by an angry word from Winnicott? Who can say? For play too—like all human endeavour—has its limits.

References

Godley, W. (2001) Saving Masud Khan. *London Review of Books*, 23(4):

Hopkins, L. (1998). D. W. Winnicott's analysis of Masud Khan. *Contemporary Psychoanalysis*, 34(1).

Hopkins, L. (2000). Masud Khan's application of Winnicott's "play" techniques to analytic consultation and treatment of adults. *Contemporary Psychoanalysis*, 56(4).

Rodman, F. R. (2003). *Winnicott: Life and Work*. Perseus Publishing House.

Sandler, A.-M. (2004). Institutional responses to boundary violations: the case of Masud Khan. *International Journal of Psychoanalysis*, 85: 27–42.